Sticker Activity Book

Team Effort

Modern Publishing
A Division of Unisystems, Inc.
New York, New York 10022

Printed in the U.S.A.
Series UPC # 69595

An Outbreak of Weird Weather

1. TRANSPORTED TO DIGIWORLD

"I've been waiting for you," says Tai's new digital partner.
Connect the dots from 1 to 21 to see him.

See Answers

Partners

"My friends call me Motimon. In fact, everyone does!"

"We're very loyal!"

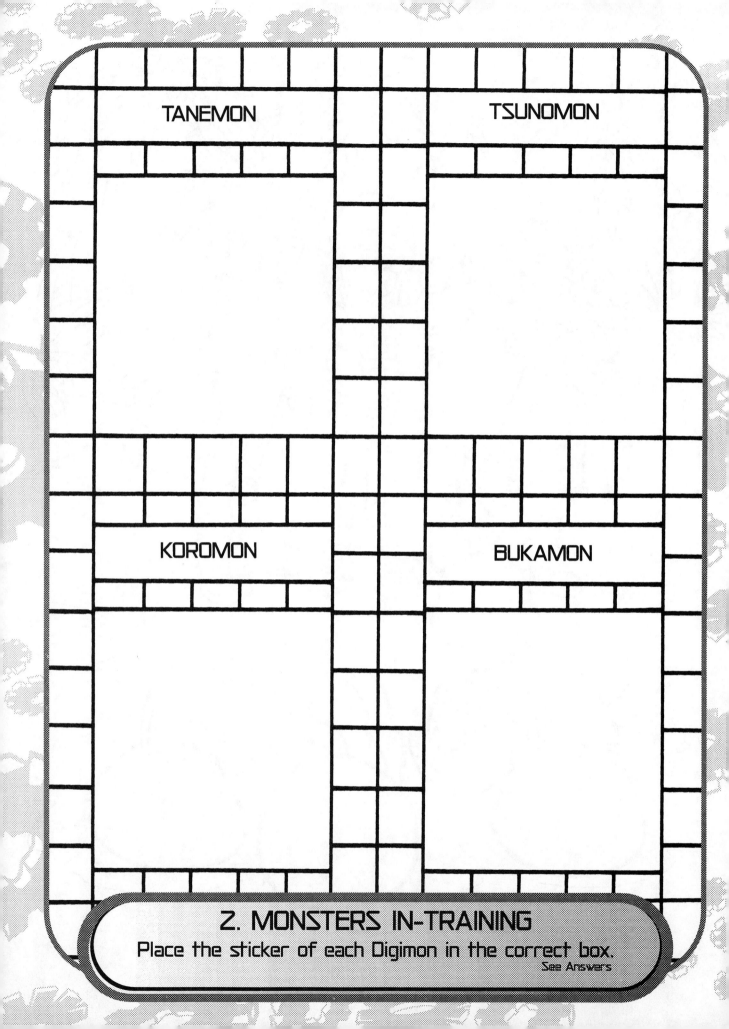

TANEMON

TSUNOMON

KOROMON

BUKAMON

2. MONSTERS IN-TRAINING
Place the sticker of each Digimon in the correct box.
See Answers

Running from an Evil Digimon

Gotta grow up sometime!

f	P	o	b	E	P
n	P	Z	E	a	R
g	o	B	a	R	j
E	m	b	A	h	q
d	T	r	r	H	z
u	k	n	d	e	n

_ _ _ _ _ _   _ _ _ _ _

3. HOT STUFF

Cross out the lowercase letters in the grid. Then write the remaining letters in the blanks to reveal Agumon's weapon.

See Answers

Super Shocker Power

4. DIGIVOLVE!
Lead each Digimon Rookie through the maze and place
the correct Digimon Champion sticker in each space.

See Answers

Unbeatable Team

Bigger, Better, Badder!

5. NEW WORLD

Nothing is common in DigiWorld! Can you find 6 Digimons In-training
in the scene? Add the sticker of the missing Digimon wherever you like.

See Answers

Too Cool for Words

The Digimon team discovers the black gear!

6. NUMEMONS—UGHH!
Color in each space that has a dot to see who is chasing Mimi and Palmon.

See Answers

Victorious Digimons

ANSWERS

1.

4.

2.

TANEMON	TSUNOMON
KOROMON	BUKAMON

5.

6.

3. PEPPER BREATH